# THE SESAME STREET TREASURY

Featuring Jim Henson's Sesame Street Muppets

## VOLUME 9

## STARRING
## THE NUMBER
## 9
## AND THE LETTERS
## M, N, AND O

Children's Television Workshop/Funk & Wagnalls, Inc.

# WRITTEN BY:

Linda Bove with the National Theatre of the Deaf
Michael Frith
Jocelyn Gunnar
Emily Perl Kingsley
Sharon Lerner
Jeffrey Moss
Liane B. Onish
Norman Stiles
Pat Tornborg
Daniel Wilcox

# ILLUSTRATED BY:

Rick Brown
Tom Cooke
Mel Crawford
Robert Dennis
Larry DiFiori
Mary Grace Eubank
Michael Frith
Dave Gantz
Joe Mathieu
Marc Nadel
Michael J. Smollin
Maggie Swanson

# PHOTOGRAPHS BY:

Neil Selkirk
View-Master International Group

Copyright © 1973, 1974, 1975, 1978, 1980, 1981, 1982, 1983 Children's Television Workshop. MUPPET Characters © 1983 Muppets Inc. All rights reserved under International and Pan-American Copyright Conventions. ® Sesame Street and the Sesame Street sign are trademarks and service marks of Children's Television Workshop. Published in the United States by Random House, Inc., New York, and simultaneously in Canada by Random House of Canada Limited, Toronto, in conjunction with the Children's Television Workshop. Distributed by Funk & Wagnalls, Inc., New York, N.Y.
Manufactured in the United States of America
4 5 6 7 8 9 0
ISBN: 0-8343-0052-4 (set); 0-8343-0061-3 (vol. 9)

# What is a magnifying glass?

What is a **magnifying glass**?
A **magnifying glass** is a special tool.
A **magnifying glass** makes things look bigger.
When you make something look bigger, you are **magnifying it**.
How do you use a **magnifying glass**?
You hold it up to your eye, and look through the glass part.
You look at whatever you want to see bigger.
What do things look like through a **magnifying glass**?
Look at the next page.

Here is a picture of
a **magnifying glass**.

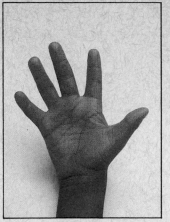

Here is a picture of somebody's hand.

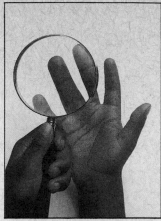

Here is a picture of the same hand through a **magnifying glass**.

Here is a picture of some stamps.

Here is a picture of the same stamps through a **magnifying glass**.

You can make your own **magnifying glass**!
Here's what you do:
Get a plain glass.
Fill it half-full of water.
Put the glass on a table.
Sit at the table so your nose is right on the edge.
Put your hand behind the glass.
Does your hand look bigger?

What other things can you look at through your **magnifying glass**?

Larry Di Fiori
Photographs by Neil Selkirk

# Action Words

**Ernie can laugh.**     **Bert can cry.**

**Bert can climb.**

**Ernie can slide.**

# ME

*As you read the poem on this page,
try to guess who is speaking.*

As I look at myself,
I like what I see.
My favorite color
Is all over me.
My feathers are yellow.
I'm happy and warm.
I'm the color of sunlight,
And the color of corn.
Who am I?

My favorite color's
The best that I've seen.
When I look in the mirror,
I see dark, hairy green.
I'm the color of grass,
And the color of trees.
I'm the color of spinach,
And the color of peas.
Who am I?

I'm happy, I'm soft,
I'm glad I'm not you.
'Cause my favorite color
Is a bright, yummy blue.
Like my good friend, small Grover,
And my friend Herry too,
When I look in a mirror,
I'm glad that I'm blue.
Who am I?

Look in a mirror. What colors are you wearing?

# MOOD FOOD

HELLO, I'M HERRY MONSTER, AND THAT MAKES ME VERY *HAPPY*, YA! BUT PEOPLE THINK IT IS HARD TO TELL WHEN I AM HAPPY, AND THAT MAKES ME SAD.

SAD

HAPPY

MAD

THEN PEOPLE SAY IT IS HARD TO TELL I AM SAD. THAT MAKES ME MAD! TO SHOW PEOPLE HOW I AM FEELING, I MAKE A SALAD. YOU, TOO, CAN SHOW PEOPLE HOW YOU ARE FEELING BY MAKING A SALAD.

## Mood Food

**What you need:**

For the face: lettuce; red cabbage; slices of cheese or meat

For the eyes: hard-boiled eggs, sliced lengthwise or across; sliced green or black olives

For the mouth: slices of melon or half of a banana, curved upward or downward; a pineapple ring (for a surprised mouth); a strawberry cut in half

For the ears: a pear cut in quarters lengthwise

For the nose and cheeks: cherries, berries, or cherry tomatoes, cut in half

For the hair: shredded carrots, cole slaw, bean or alfalfa sprouts

**What you do:**
Just place the ingredients of your choice together to make a face that shows your mood

# Nn

## Oscar's Favorite N Word

I'm Oscar the Grouch and I'm going to show you something that starts with the letter **N**! Heh, heh. Just turn the page.

It's NOTHING!
**Nothing** starts with the
letter **N**, and **nothing** is all I'm
gonna show you in this book,
'cause I hate the yucchy alphabet!
Now don't bother me
any more. Good-by!

Nothing?

Nothing.

Nope.
Nothing.

Nothing.
Nothing.
Nothing.

# Herry Monster

| | |
|---|---|
| **Home:** | 456 Sesame Street |
| **Favorite Food:** | Monster muffins |
| **Favorite Drink:** | Monster malted |
| **Best Friend:** | Prairie Dawn |
| **Pet:** | Fuzzy the Kitten |
| **Pet Peeve:** | Chairs that break when he sits in them |
| **Favorite Activities:** | Lifting barbells, growing pretty flowers |
| **Favorite Saying:** | "Family dinners are really great. We eat the food and then the plate." |

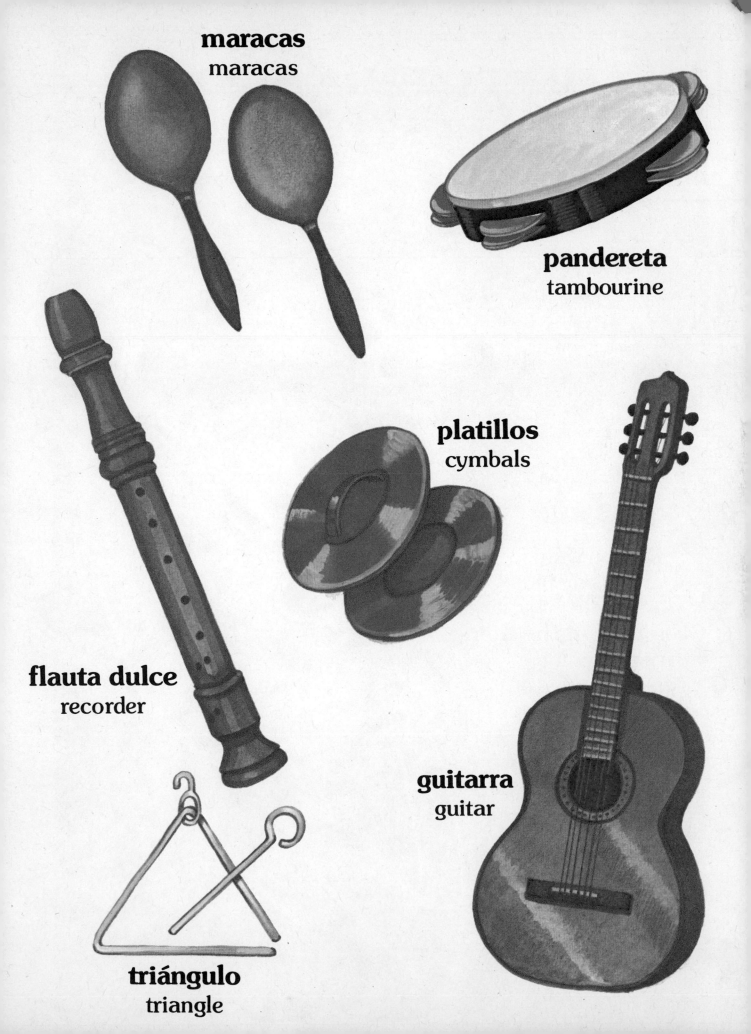

**maracas**
maracas

**pandereta**
tambourine

**platillos**
cymbals

**flauta dulce**
recorder

**guitarra**
guitar

**triángulo**
triangle

9
Do you want to have some fun? Come fly with me, and we will count the flying saucers. 1...2...3...4...5 ...6...7...8...9! Nine flying saucers! Oh, it is marvelous!

During his summer vacation at the beach Ernie decided to take swimming lessons. And what a wonderful instructor he had! Octavia Octopus, champion swimmer, taught Ernie to do the breaststroke, the backstroke, the crawl, and the butterfly. She taught him how to tread water and how to swim very fast and for a very long time. Octavia told Ernie that there was only one problem with his style—not enough arms!

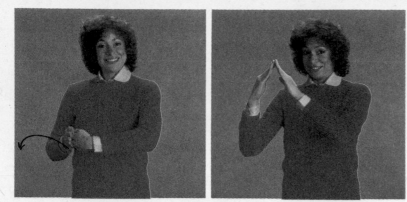

neighborhood

# People in the Neighborhood

grocer

policeman

letter carrier

sanitation worker

plumber

dentist

barber

# How many things in this picture can you "sign"?

Be careful crossing streets.

Don't

cross

the street

when

the traffic light is red!

# The Mystery of the Missing Hat

I'm looking up! I'm looking down!
I'm looking for the color **brown**!

I'm looking for it everywhere!
Ah-ha! I see a big **brown** bear!

A big **brown** bear with big **brown** shoes . . .
Uh-oh! I think he's got the blues.

Excuse me, Bear, but why the tears?
The big **brown** bear cries, "It's my ears!"

"They're cold without my big **brown** hat—
I lost it (sniff) and that is that."

Oh, don't be sad—for help is here!
We'll find your big **brown** hat—don't fear.

We're looking up! We're looking down!
We're looking for a hat that's **brown**!

Can you find the **brown** hat in the picture?

# The Story of the Nine Dragons

Once upon a time, in the faraway kingdom of St. George, there lived a baseball team. There were 9 players on the team.

One day, as they reached their practice field, **9** dragons leaped out of the woods, breathing fire and smoke and yelling, *"Arkle-Snarkle Higgeldy Snoo!"*

This frightened the baseball players and they ran away. After all, you'd be frightened, too, if **9** dragons leaped out of the woods while you were playing baseball.

Every day when the **9** baseball players got to the ball field the same thing would happen.

After this had gone on for several weeks, one of the players decided it was time to do something about the dragons.

"I've got an idea how to get rid of those dragons," he said. And he told his idea to the other players.

So the next day, each of the **9** players got a big feather and went out to the baseball field.

When the **9** dragons jumped out of the forest, the **9** players took the **9** feathers and tickled the **9** dragons on their tummies. The dragons rolled over on their backs and giggled dragon-giggles and kicked their feet in the air.

But when they were finished being tickled, the dragons jumped up and breathed fire and smoke and yelled, *"Arkle-Snarkle Higgeldy Snoo,"* and frightened the players away again.

So the 9 baseball players decided that tickling the dragons wasn't such a good idea after all.

Suddenly, the team's right fielder (who also happened to be a dragon expert) stepped forward.

"I just happen to be a dragon expert," she said, "and I have an idea. Here's my dragon book. Why don't we look in it and see what *Arkle-Snarkle Higgeldy Snoo* means?"

"It's so crazy it just might work," said the third baseman.

The next day, when the **9** baseball players went out to the field, they pulled behind them a great big wagon with a cover over it.

Once again the **9** dragons jumped out of the woods, breathed fire and smoke, and yelled, *"Arkle-Snarkle Higgeldy Snoo! Arkle-Snarkle Higgeldy Snoo!!"*

The players quickly pulled the cover off the wagon and, lo and behold, there were **9** great big dragon-sized baseball caps, **9** great big dragon-sized baseball mitts, and **9** great big dragon-sized baseball bats!

For the right fielder's dragon book had told them that *"Arkle-Snarkle Higgeldy Snoo"* is dragon-talk for, "We want to play baseball, too!"

So every day the **9** baseball players went out to the baseball field and met the **9** dragons on the dragon team...and they played baseball.

So if you happen to be walking through the woods one day and **9** dragons jump out at you, breathing fire and smoke and yelling, *"Arkle-Snarkle Higgeldy Snoo,"* don't be afraid. Chances are they just want to play baseball!

# o O Grover Knows His O's

Hello.

I, Grover, am going to tell you some poems all about three friends of mine. And their names all begin with the letter **O**.

I like Ogden Ox . . .
he really is neat.

Except when he's dancing
and steps on my feet.

Olive the Octopus
has many charms.

Except when she hugs me
with all of her arms.

Ollie the Ostrich
is very well bred.

Except when he's tired
and sits on my head.

Well, those are all the **O** poems
I have time for today. I do not
think I am going to do any more
for a long, long time. Good-by.
O o o o o o o o o o o o o h.

### THE MOUSE AND THE CLOCK

Hickory, dickory, dock!
The mouse ran up the clock;
The clock struck one,
And down he run,
Hickory, dickory, dock!